Music and Lyrics by **Dolly Parton**

Cover artwork courtesy of SpotCo
Back cover photo by Justin Stephens

ISBN 978-1-4234-9384-6

HAL•LEONARD®
CORPORATION

7777 W. BLUEMOUND RD. P.O. BOX 13819 MILWAUKEE, WI 53213

In Australia Contact:
Hal Leonard Australia Pty. Ltd.
4 Lentara Court
Cheltenham, Victoria, 3192 Australia
Email: ausadmin@halleonard.com.au

Visit Hal Leonard Online at
www.halleonard.com

present

Music and Lyrics by
DOLLY PARTON

Book by
PATRICIA RESNICK

BASED ON THE 20TH CENTURY FOX PICTURE

STARRING

ALLISON JANNEY

STEPHANIE J. BLOCK

MEGAN HILTY

KATHY FITZGERALD   **ANDY KARL**

AND

MARC KUDISCH

with

IOANA ALFONSO   TIMOTHY GEORGE ANDERSON   JENNIFER BALAGNA   JUSTIN BOHON
PAUL CASTREE   DAN COONEY   JEREMY DAVIS   GAELEN GILLILAND   AUTUMN GUZZARDI
ANN HARADA   NEIL HASKELL   LISA HOWARD   VAN HUGHES   MICHAEL X. MARTIN
MICHAEL MINDLIN   KAREN MURPHY   MARK MYARS   JUSTIN PATTERSON   JESSICA LEA PATTY
CHARLIE POLLOCK   TORY ROSS   WAYNE SCHRODER   MAIA NKENGE WILSON   BRANDI WOOTEN

Scenic Design	Costume Design	Lighting Design	Sound Design
SCOTT PASK	WILLIAM IVEY LONG	JULES FISHER & KENNETH POSNER	JOHN H. SHIVERS

Casting	Imaging	Hair Design	Make-Up Design
TELSEY + COMPANY	PETER NIGRINI & PEGGY EISENHAUER	PAUL HUNTLEY & EDWARD J. WILSON	ANGELINA AVALLONE

Technical Supervisor	Scenic Design Associate	Production Supervisor	Associate Director	Associate Choreographer
NEIL A. MAZZELLA	EDWARD PIERCE	WILLIAM JOSEPH BARNES	DAVE SOLOMON	RACHEL BRESS

General Management	Press Agent	Marketing	Music Coordinator
NINA LANNAN ASSOCIATES	THE HARTMAN GROUP	TYPE A MARKETING SITUATION INTERACTIVE	MICHAEL KELLER

Orchestrator	Additional Orchestrations & Incidental Music Arrangements	Dance Music Arrangements	Additional Music Arrangements
BRUCE COUGHLIN	STEPHEN OREMUS & ALEX LACAMOIRE	ALEX LACAMOIRE	KEVIN STITES & CHARLES duCHATEAU

Music Direction and Vocal Arrangements by
STEPHEN OREMUS

Produced by
ROBERT GREENBLATT

Choreographed by
ANDY BLANKENBUEHLER

Directed by
JOE MANTELLO

Allison Janney as Violet Newstead

Stephanie J. Block as Judy Bernly

Megan Hilty as Doralee Rhodes

Marc Kudisch as Franklin Hart, Jr.

© Joan Marcus

© Joan Marcus

© Joan Marcus

© Joan Marcus

Photo by Justin Stephens

Photo by Justin Stephens

NINE TO FIVE

Words and Music by DOLLY PARTON
Vocal Arrangement by STEPHEN OREMUS
Piano Arrangement by STEPHEN OREMUS
and ALEX LACAMOIRE

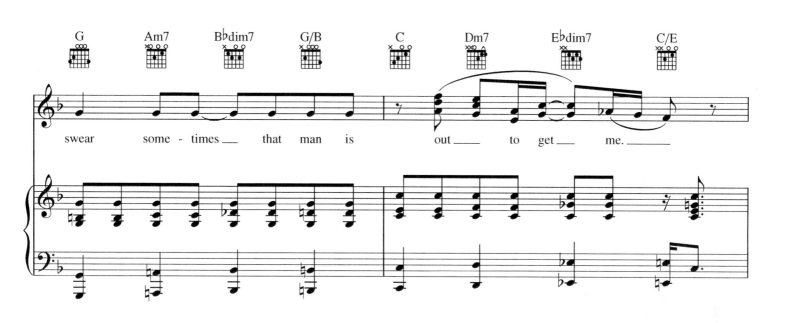

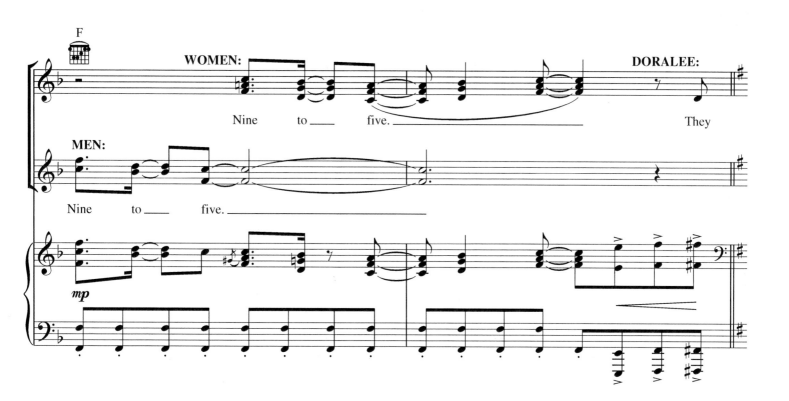

AROUND HERE

Words and Music by DOLLY PARTON
Piano/Vocal Arrangement by STEPHEN OREMUS

HERE FOR YOU

Words and Music by DOLLY PARTON
Piano Arrangement by STEPHEN OREMUS
and ALEX LACAMOIRE

I JUST MIGHT

Words and Music by DOLLY PARTON
Vocal Arrangement by STEPHEN OREMUS
Piano Arrangement by STEPHEN OREMUS
and ALEX LACAMOIRE

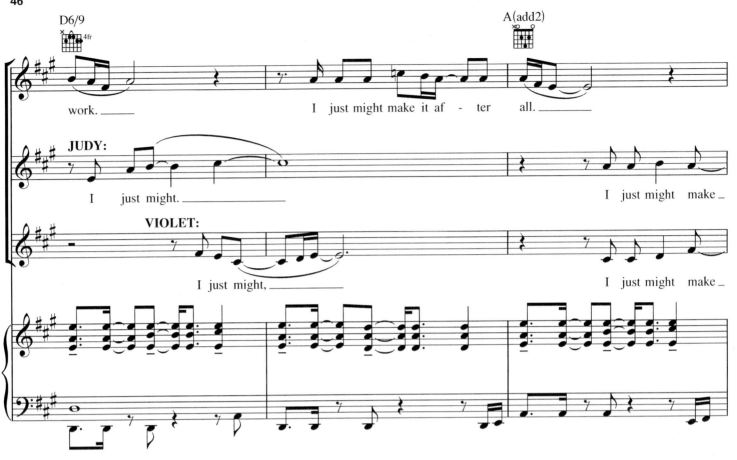

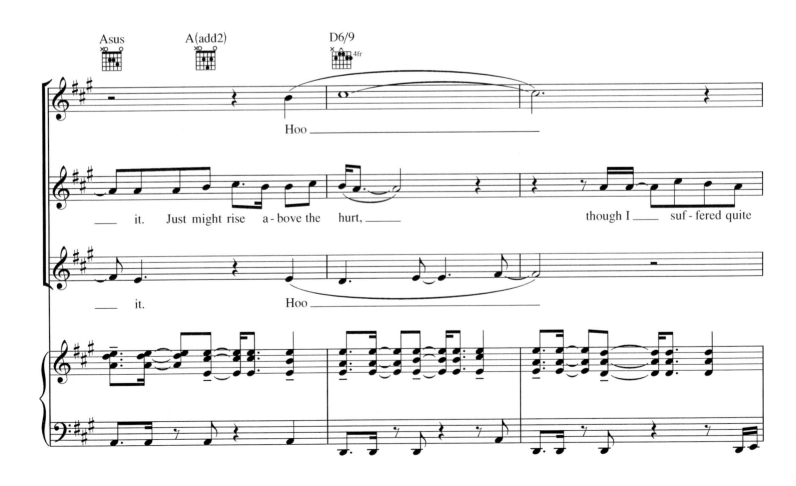

BACKWOODS BARBIE

Words and Music by DOLLY PARTON
Vocal Arrangement by STEPHEN OREMUS

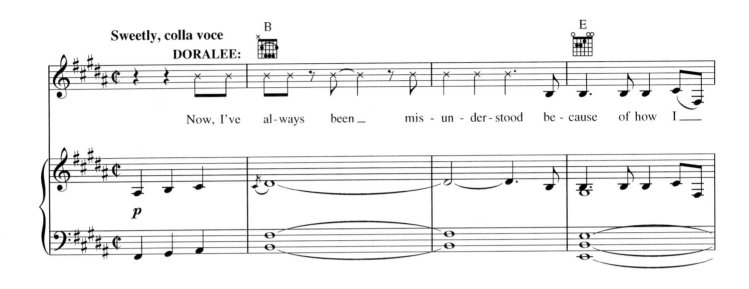

Now, I've al-ways been _ mis-un-der-stood be-cause of how I _

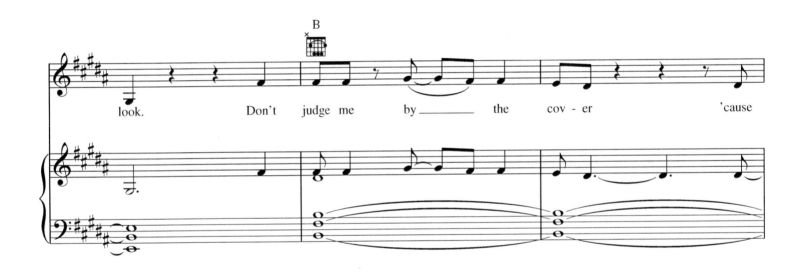

look. Don't judge me by _ the cov-er 'cause

I'm a real good _ book. _ So read in-to it what _

HEART TO HART

Words and Music by DOLLY PARTON
Vocal Arrangement by STEPHEN OREMUS
Piano Arrangement by STEPHEN OREMUS
and ALEX LACAMOIRE

dam. And if I ev-er turn loose, I'll tell you the truth, dear

Hart, you won't be quite the same. ___ And if I ev-er get my

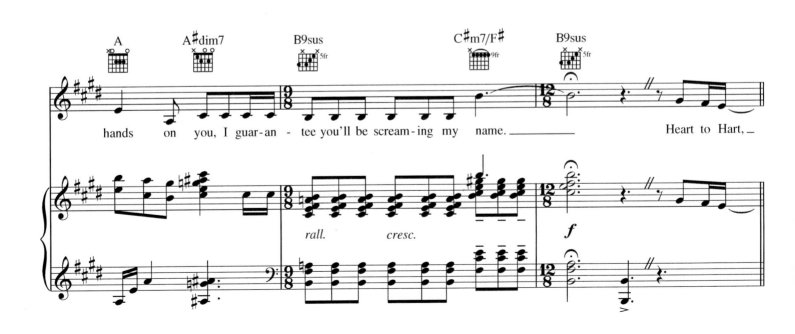

hands on you, I guar-an-tee you'll be scream-ing my name. ___ Heart to Hart, ___

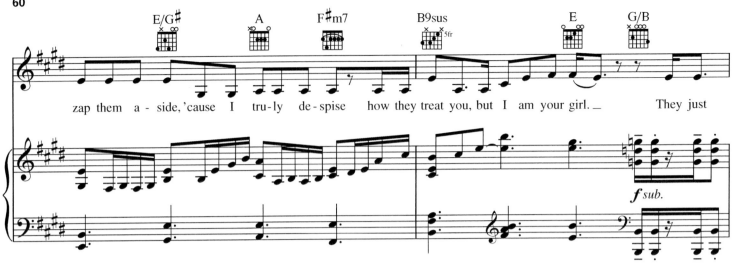

zap them a-side, 'cause I tru-ly de-spise how they treat you, but I am your girl. __ They just

don't un-der-stand what a won-der-ful man I've come to know you to be. __ And

I have a feel-ing that deep down in-side, you might just feel the same a-bout me. Heart to Hart, __

ENSEMBLE:

Hoo _____ hoo _____ ah _____ Heart to Hart, __

with pedal

SHINE LIKE THE SUN

Words and Music by DOLLY PARTON
Vocal Arrangement by STEPHEN OREMUS
Piano Arrangement by STEPHEN OREMUS
and ALEX LACAMOIRE

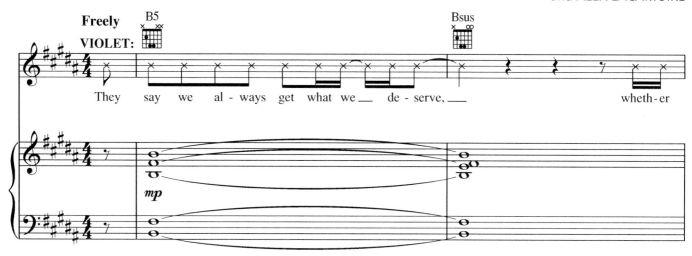

VIOLET: They say we al-ways get what we de-serve, wheth-er

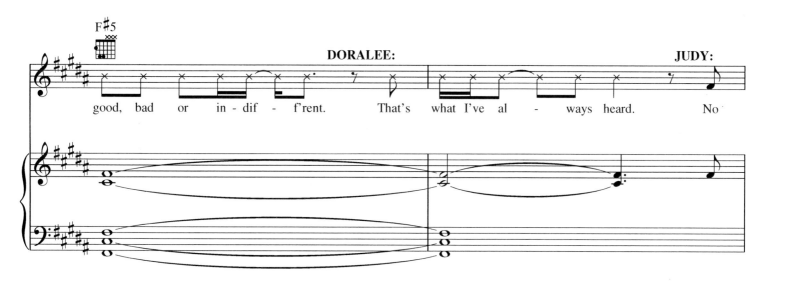

DORALEE: good, bad or in-dif-f'rent. That's what I've al-ways heard.

JUDY: No

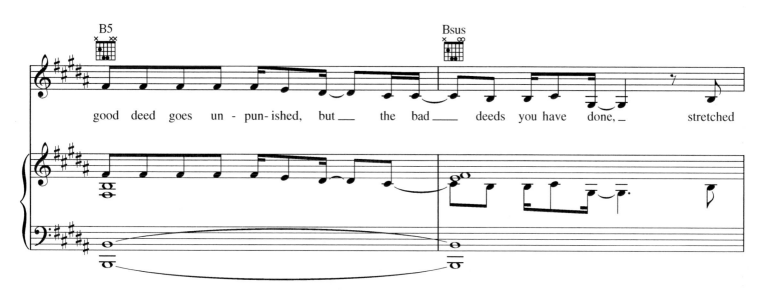

good deed goes un-pun-ished, but the bad deeds you have done, stretched

* The ensemble continues singing with the leads

ONE OF THE BOYS

Words and Music by DOLLY PARTON
Vocal Arrangement by STEPHEN OREMUS
Piano Arrangement by ALEX LACAMOIRE

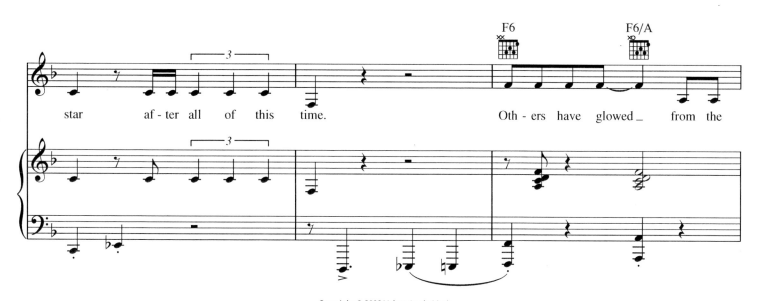

5 TO 9

Words and Music by
DOLLY PARTON

CHANGE IT

Words and Music by DOLLY PARTON
Vocal Arrangement by STEPHEN OREMUS
Piano Arrangement by STEPHEN OREMUS
and ALEX LACAMOIRE

LET LOVE GROW

Words and Music by DOLLY PARTON
Vocal Arrangement by STEPHEN OREMUS

104

GET OUT AND STAY OUT

Words and Music by DOLLY PARTON
Piano Arrangement by STEPHEN OREMUS
and ALEX LACAMOIRE

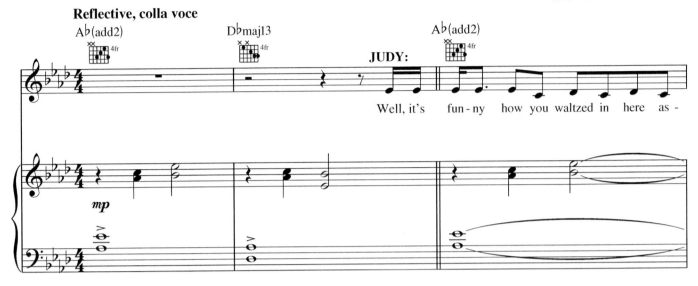

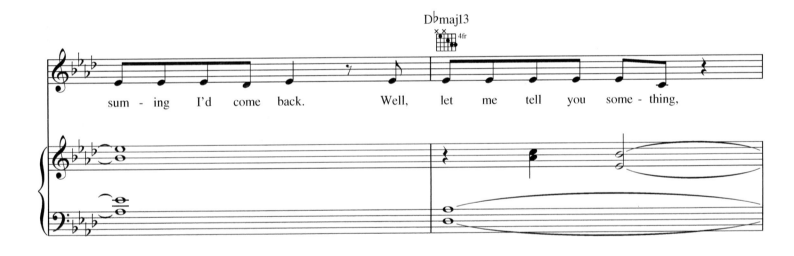

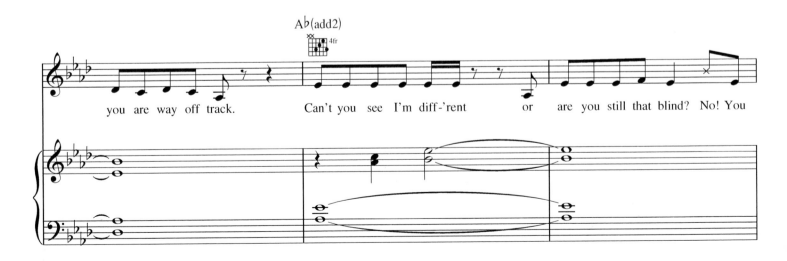

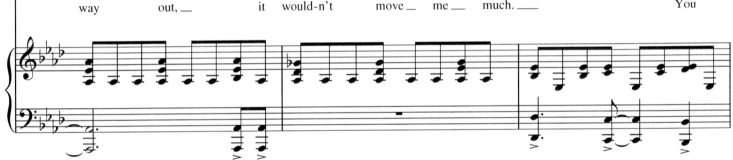

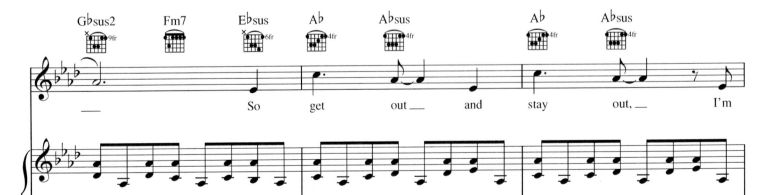